Contents

Any words appearing in the text in bold, **like this**, are explained in the Glossary

Hundreds, tens and units

0 1 2 3 4 5 6 7 8 9

▲ *The ten digits 0 to 9*

A **digit** is a symbol, 0 to 9, used to write a number.

To write the number six hundred and ninety-two, you need three digits: 692

356 is a three-digit number.
The digit 3 shows how many hundreds there are,
the digit 5 shows how many tens
and the digit 6 shows how many units, or ones.

So, 356 is 300 and 50 and 6.

What does it mean?

4295 is a four-digit number.
The digit 4 shows how many thousands there are.

Use your head

Say the missing numbers.

543 = 500 + ? + 3
4608 = 4000 + ? + 8

? Question
What sort of
numbers are
these?

238941

What does it mean?

A spike **abacus** is used to show numbers, and also to add, subtract, multiply or divide numbers. The number of beads on each spike match the digit in that place.

Use your head

Make 24 different three-digit numbers using these four digit cards.

TIP Start by finding all those with '1' in the hundreds place, then '2' in the hundreds place, and so on.

| 1 | 7 | 5 | | 5 | 1 | 2 |

▲ *Digital watches show the time using digits.*

Play the digit game

This is a game for several players. You need digit cards 0 to 9, placed in a hat, and a 3-digit number board for each player. Take turns to draw a card from the hat. All players write the first number in either their hundreds, their tens or their units place. Then draw a second card. Players write this number in one of their remaining two positions. Finally draw a third card, and this number is written in the last place.

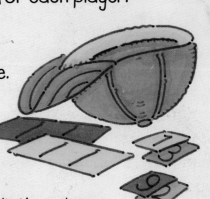

The winner is the player with the largest 3-digit number.

Estimating and rounding

An **estimate** is a rough guess.

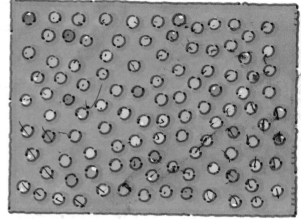

? **Question**

How many counters do you think are in this picture?

Do you think there are about 10, about 50, about 100, or about 1000? The number you choose is called your estimate.

There are exactly 107 counters, so 'about 100' is a good estimate.

Play the estimation game

This is a game for several players. You need about 100 counters or cubes placed in a bag.

- Tip a pile of counters onto the table. Each player writes an estimate of the number of counters in the pile.
- Next, count the exact number together, collecting them in tens.
- Find out how close each estimate is by working out the difference between each estimate and the exact number.
- The winner is the player with the closest estimate.
- Replace the counters in the bag and play again.

What does it mean?

A **number line** is a line with 'divisions' or 'markings' which are numbered in order.

▼ *The number 48 lies between 40 and 50. Its nearest ten is fifty. 48 **rounded** to its nearest 10 is 50.*

40   41   42   43   44   45   46   47   48   49   50

What does it mean?

Rounding a number is a way of saying the rough size of the number. When you say the rough size of the number it is called an **approximation**.

Use your head

Round these numbers, first to their nearest 100, and then to their nearest 10.

For example, 146 can be rounded to 100 or 150.

ZOO
72 km

NEW TOWN
323 km

THEME PARK
178 km

What does it mean?

When you round to the nearest 10 …
- below the number: this is called rounding down.
- above the number: this is called rounding up.

When a number such as 165 is exactly mid-way between 160 and 170, then you always round up.

Some number lines have all their markings numbered. Others only have some markings numbered.

| 0 | 1 | 2 | 3 | 4 | 5 | 6 | 7 | 8 | 9 | 10 |

| 50 | 55 | 60 | 65 | 70 | 75 | 80 | 85 | 90 | 95 | 100 |

| 0 | 10 | 20 | 30 | 40 | 50 | 60 | 70 | 80 | 90 | 100 |

| 300 | | | | | | | | | 400 |

▼ *A ruler is a type of number line.*

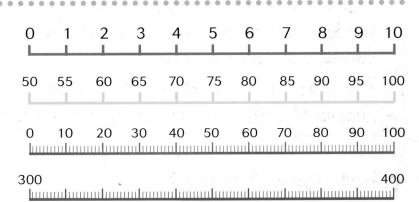

Simple fractions

When something is divided into equal parts,
the parts are called **fractions**. If there are ...

- two equal parts, each is called one **half**, written $\frac{1}{2}$
- three equal parts, each is called one **third**, written $\frac{1}{3}$
- four equal parts, each is called one **quarter**, written $\frac{1}{4}$
- five equal parts, each is called one **fifth**, written $\frac{1}{5}$

? Question

What fractions have these
shapes been divided into?

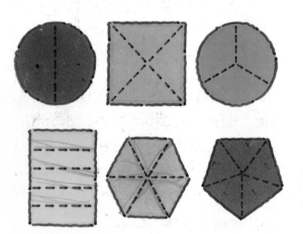

? Question

What fractions can you see here?

Play the fraction game

Make a dice by writing $\frac{1}{2}$, $\frac{1}{2}$, $\frac{1}{3}$, $\frac{1}{3}$, $\frac{1}{4}$, $\frac{1}{6}$
on the faces of a cube. Each player
draws three 3 x 4 rectangles on
squared paper.

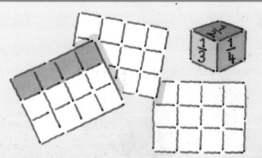

Take turns to throw the dice, and colour that fraction
of one of your rectangles, e.g. throw $\frac{1}{3}$, and colour one third
of one rectangle. Check each other's colouring. The winner
is the first player to completely colour all three rectangles.

Draw three more rectangles each and play again.

As the minute hand of a clock turns, it traces fractions of an hour.

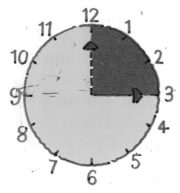

▲ 15 minutes have passed, or a quarter hour.

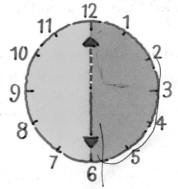

▲ 30 minutes have passed, or a half hour.

Fun to do

Make a 'fraction show'. You need two paper plates or paper circles of different colours. Use scissors to cut each in a straight line to its centre.

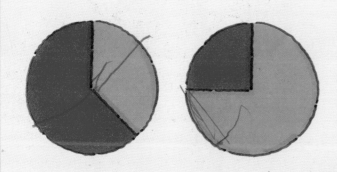

The two plates can now be joined by sliding one to link with the other at the cuts. Keep one plate held firmly, and gently turn the other to show different fractions. What fractions can you show?

Use your head

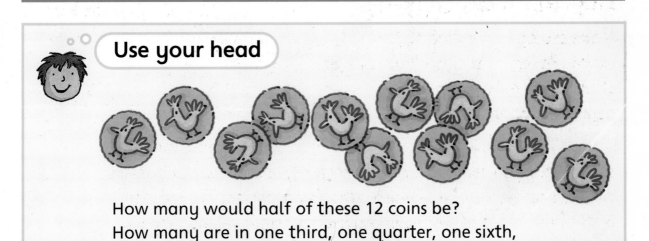

How many would half of these 12 coins be?
How many are in one third, one quarter, one sixth, and one twelfth of all the coins?

More fractions

◀ *This slice of cake is one **quarter** of the whole cake. The whole cake has four quarters, so there are three quarters left.*

The number on the bottom part of the **fraction** is called the **denominator**. It shows how many equal parts something has been divided into.

The number on the top part of the fraction is called the **numerator**. It shows how many of the equal parts are in the fraction.

The fraction $\frac{1}{4}$ has a numerator of 1, and a denominator of 4. It means one out of four equal parts.

The fraction $\frac{3}{4}$ has a numerator of 3, and a denominator of 4. It means three out of four equal parts.

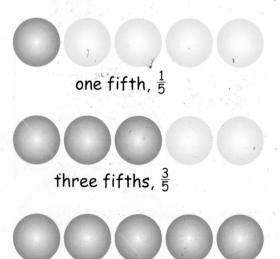

one fifth, $\frac{1}{5}$

two fifths, $\frac{2}{5}$

three fifths, $\frac{3}{5}$

four fifths, $\frac{4}{5}$

five fifths, $\frac{5}{5}$

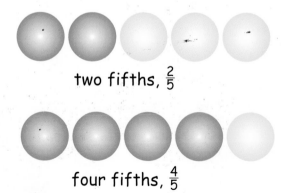

▲ *The red balls in these sets of five balls show different fractions. Each fraction is a number of **fifths**.*

Use your head

What fraction of each of these rectangle shapes has been coloured?

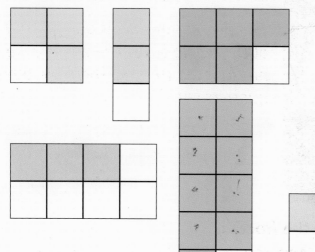

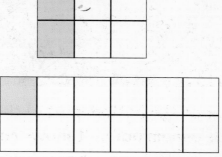

Use your head

What fraction of these faces are: happy, sad, wearing a hat, not wearing a hat, wearing a moustache, not wearing a moustache, wearing glasses, not wearing glasses?

Equivalent fractions

? Question

Look at these cut up flapjacks.
Is there any difference between
choosing one **half** of a flapjack,
or two **quarters** of a flapjack?

What does it mean?

When two **fractions** are the same amount, they are called **equivalent**.

$\frac{1}{2}$ and $\frac{2}{4}$ of the flapjack are the same amount.

So, $\frac{1}{2}$ and $\frac{2}{4}$ are called **equivalent fractions**.

$\frac{3}{6}$ are yellow, or $\frac{1}{2}$ are yellow.

$\frac{1}{2}$ and $\frac{3}{6}$ are equivalent fractions.

$\frac{2}{6}$ are blue, or $\frac{1}{3}$ are blue.

$\frac{1}{3}$ and $\frac{2}{6}$ are equivalent fractions.

What does it mean?

A **fraction wall** is a chart which helps you to see equivalent fractions.

Use your head

What pairs of equivalent fractions can you see in the fraction wall?

one whole							
$\frac{1}{2}$				$\frac{1}{2}$			
$\frac{1}{4}$		$\frac{1}{4}$		$\frac{1}{4}$		$\frac{1}{4}$	
$\frac{1}{8}$	$\frac{1}{8}$	$\frac{1}{8}$	$\frac{1}{8}$	$\frac{1}{8}$	$\frac{1}{8}$	$\frac{1}{8}$	$\frac{1}{8}$

TIP A **multiplication square** helps you to find sets of equivalent fractions.

For example, to find fractions equivalent to $\frac{1}{3}$, look along the '1-row' and the '3-row' to match the **numerator** and **denominator** of the fraction.

From here you can read sets of fractions equivalent to $\frac{1}{3}$:
$\frac{1}{3}, \frac{2}{6}, \frac{3}{9}, \frac{4}{12}, \frac{5}{15}, \dots$

1	2	3	4	5	6	7	8	9	10
2	4	6	8	10	12	14	16	18	20
3	6	9	12	15	18	21	24	27	30
4	8	12	16	20	24	28	32	36	40
5	10	15	20	25	30	35	40	45	50
6	12	18	24	30	36	42	48	54	60
7	14	21	28	35	42	49	56	63	70
8	16	24	32	40	48	56	64	72	80
9	18	27	36	45	54	63	72	81	90
10	20	30	40	50	60	70	80	90	100

Use your head

Say a fraction which is equivalent to each of these:

$\frac{2}{3}$ $\frac{3}{5}$ $\frac{3}{4}$ $\frac{1}{6}$ $\frac{4}{5}$

Try first without looking at the multiplication square, then look to check if you are correct.

Play the equivalent fraction game

Play this game in pairs. One player secretly writes a fraction with numerator and denominator each less than 8, such as $\frac{2}{5}$, then says the fraction, 'two fifths'. The other player has to write, then say, an equivalent fraction, such as $\frac{4}{10}$, 'four tenths'. Check the answer by using the multiplication square. Swap roles and play several rounds.

Decimal fractions

One tenth and one hundredth are more examples of **fractions**.

One tenth is one part out of ten equal parts.

One hundredth is one part out of a hundred equal parts.

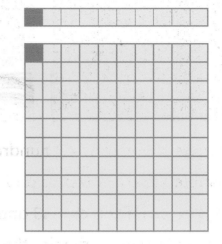

The **number line** from 1 to 10 can be split into tenths.

Imagine that the line between 4 and 5 can be split into tenths.

Three parts along the line shows the position 'four whole numbers and three tenths' or $4\frac{3}{10}$.

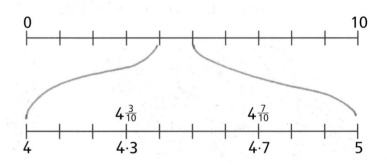

What does it mean?

You often write $4\frac{3}{10}$ as 4·3, which you read as 'four point three'.

4·3 is called a **decimal number**.

The point is called a **decimal point**.

The decimal point splits the number into whole numbers and tenths.

▶ *A **centimetre** is divided into tenths. The matchstick measures 4·7 centimetres, that is 4 centimetres and 7 tenths of a centimetre.*

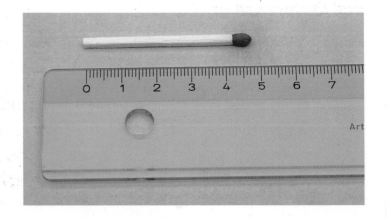

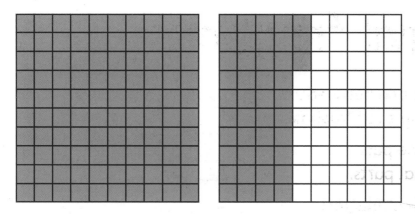

1 whole square and 43 hundredths are coloured, or

1 whole square, 4 tenths and 3 hundredths are coloured.

You can write this as 1·43 and say 'one point four three'.

The decimal point divides the whole numbers from the tenths and the hundredths.

▲ Each 10p coin is one tenth of a pound.

Each 1p coin is one hundredth of a pound.

We write £1·43

The decimal point divides the pounds (1) from the tenths (4) and the hundredths (3).

Use your head

Read each number as a fraction and as a decimal number.

hundreds	tens	units	•	tenths	hundredths
	3	4	•	6	
		3	•	7	
		1	•	4	2
	1	0	•	3	5

Play the decimal money game

This is a game for several players. Use nine each of 1p, 10p and £1 coins. Put them in a bag, and take a handful of coins each. Write and say how much you each have, using the decimal point. Who has the most money? Replace the coins and repeat the game several times.

15

Percentages

A **percentage** is a fraction with a **denominator** of 100.

'**Per cent**' means 'out of a hundred'.

% is a short way of writing 'per cent'.

So we read 30% as 'thirty per cent' and mean 'thirty out of one hundred' or $\frac{30}{100}$.

$\frac{60}{100}$ or 60% of the pegs are green. ▶

$\frac{30}{100}$ or 30% are yellow.

$\frac{10}{100}$ or 10% are pink.

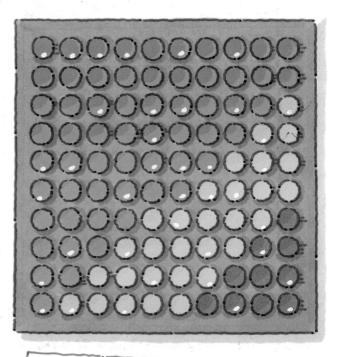

▶ *Look at this piece of story. It contains 100 words.*

There are ? 1-letter words, so ?% are 1-letter words.

There are ? 2-letter words so ?% are 2-letter words.

There are ? 5-letter words so ?% are 5-letter words.

Use your head

What percentage of the words have:
3 letters, 4 letters?

I crept through the narrow gate to the playground at the back of the school, then stopped and looked around. There was no one there – everyone was inside. I tiptoed along the path to the bicycle shed and listened. Everything was quiet.

The door of the shed was closed. I slowly pushed the door open and tried to peer inside. The smell of dust and old bike oil greeted me, but I still couldn't see anything. I opened the door a little wider to let in more light. As my eyes adjusted to the gloom, I finally saw the bike.

It is useful to know the percentages which match some common **fractions**. For example:

One **half** of the pieces of fruit are pears.
50% of the fruit are pears.

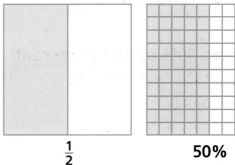

$\frac{1}{2}$ **50%**

One **quarter** of the apples are red.
25% of the apples are red.

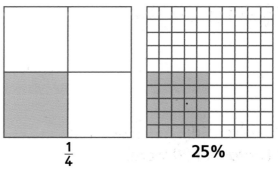

$\frac{1}{4}$ **25%**

Three quarters of the apples are green.
75% of the apples are green.

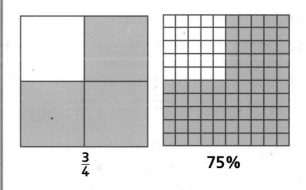

$\frac{3}{4}$ **75%**

Play the percentage game

This is a game for two players. Use different coins which total £1, for example one 20p coin, five 10p coins, four 5p coins, three 2p coins, and four 1p coins. Put them in a bag, and take turns to take a handful. Each player guesses what percentage of the total has been taken. The handful is then counted to see whose guess was closest. Play several rounds.

Change the game by placing coins worth £2 or 50p in the bag.

Positive and negative numbers

'Ten, nine, eight, seven, six, five, four, three, two, one, zero, ...'

These are the numbers we say as we count back from ten.

We do not have to stop the count at zero. The numbers less than zero are called negative numbers. We say 'negative one, negative two, negative three, ... and so on.

What does it mean?

A number less than zero is called a **negative number**.

We write −3, which we read as negative three, or sometimes **minus** three.

A number more than zero is called a **positive number**.

We write +4, which we read as positive four, or sometimes **plus** four.

| −4 | −3 | −2 | −1 | 0 | +1 | +2 | +3 | +4 | +5 | +6 |

On a warm day the **temperature** is about 20° Celsius. When the weather gets colder, the temperature falls. Water turns to ice when the temperature falls to 0° Celsius. If the temperature turns colder still, it falls to −1° Celsius, then −2° Celsius, and so on.

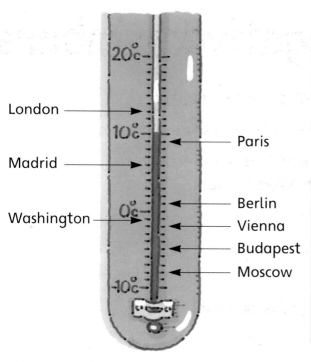

London

Madrid

Washington

Paris

Berlin
Vienna
Budapest
Moscow

◀ *Temperature varies from place to place. Different places around the world have different temperatures. These are the temperatures of places at the same time.*

Use your head

What are the temperatures in: Vienna, Paris, Moscow, Madrid, Budapest?

This pop chart shows that 'Angel on my mind' was tenth last week, and is now top. This means that it has climbed 9 places in the charts: its change is +9. 'Red sunset' was first last week, but is now third, so it has fallen two places and its change is −2. ▼

Use your head

Look at the pop chart below. Which other songs have fallen?

This week	Last week	Change	Title	Sung by
1	10	+9	Angel on my mind	Mel James
2	4	+2	Who lied?	The G-Boys
3	1	−2	Red sunset	Kiko
4	2	−2	Billie	Mary
5	8	+3	In love with you	The Thursdays
6	9	+3	Tears in my eyes	Terri Fred
7	7		Don't go	The Nice Girls
8	5	−3	My present	Girlzone
9	12	+3	Pillow dreams	Twilight
10	3	−7	Crazy Baby	Claudette

Multiples

When you start at zero, and count in fours, the numbers you say are: four, eight, twelve, sixteen, …

Can you say any more?

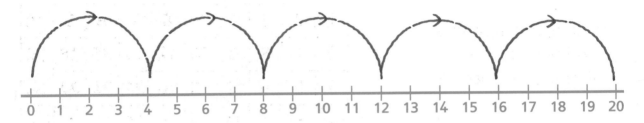

0 1 2 3 4 5 6 7 8 9 10 11 12 13 14 15 16 17 18 19 20

▲ *These are the numbers you land on when you jump in fours.*

What does it mean?

The numbers in the fours are called the **multiples** of 4.

The multiples of 4 are: 4, 8, 12, 16, 20, 24, 28, 32, 36, 40, …

The fifth multiple of 4 is 20.

The seventh multiple of 4 is 28.

▶ *Another way of finding the multiples of 4, is to write the numbers in a 4-column grid. The multiples of 4 appear on the right. The multiples of 4 are the numbers in the ×4 multiplication table.*

1	2	3	4
5	6	7	8
9	10	11	12
13	14	15	16
17	18	19	20
21	22	23	24
25	26	27	28
29	30	31	32
33	34	35	36
37	38	39	40

$1 \times 4 = 4$

$2 \times 4 = 8$

$3 \times 4 = 12$

$4 \times 4 = 16$

$5 \times 4 = 20$

$6 \times 4 = 24$

$7 \times 4 = 28$

$8 \times 4 = 32$

$9 \times 4 = 36$

$10 \times 4 = 40$

To find the multiples of 6, complete a 6-column grid.

The multiples of 2 are: 2, 4, 6, 8, 10, 12, 14, 16, 18, 20, ...

Notice that the multiples of 2 are the even numbers.

The multiples of 3 are: 3, 6, 9, 12, 15, 18, 21, 24, 27, 30, ...

Notice that the multiples of 3 are odd, even, odd, even, odd, even, ... They are alternately odd and even.

A **multiplication square** shows the multiples of different numbers.

1	2	3	4	5	6	7	8	9	10
2	4	6	8	10	12	14	16	18	20
3	6	9	12	15	18	21	24	27	30
4	8	12	16	20	24	28	32	36	40
5	10	15	20	25	30	35	40	45	50
6	12	18	24	30	36	42	48	54	60
7	14	21	28	35	42	49	56	63	70
8	16	24	32	40	48	56	64	72	80
9	18	27	36	45	54	63	72	81	90
10	20	30	40	50	60	70	80	90	100

▶ *This multiplication square is marked to show how the multiples of 4 appear in both the 4th row and the 4th column.*

What does it mean?

12 is a multiple of 2.

12 is also a multiple of 3.

12 is a **common multiple** of 2 and 3.

? Question

Look at this chart. Can you spot the common multiples of 2 and of 3?

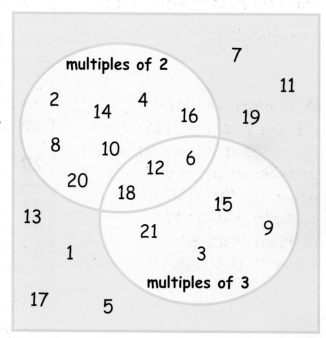

Factors

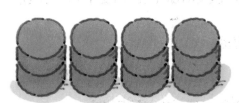  

▲ 8 counters can be grouped in 2s.
8 can be divided by 2.

▲ 8 counters can be grouped in 4s.
8 can be divided by 4.

▲ 8 counters can be grouped in 8s.
8 can be divided by 8.

8 counters can also be grouped in 1s.

So, 8 can be divided by 1, by 2, by 4 and by 8.

These numbers are called the **factors** of 8.

The factors of 8 are 1, 2, 4 and 8.

What does it mean?

The factors of a number are those which will divide into it exactly.

Play the factor game

This is a game for two players. Choose any number, for example 16. Shuffle a set of numbered cards, 1 to 10, and deal five each. The players lay out all of their cards which are factors of 16 and collect 1 counter for each card they have laid out. Pick up all the cards, reshuffle, choose a different number and play again. The winner is the player with most counters after 10 rounds.

◄ *12 chairs can be arranged in 3 rows of 4, so 12 = 3 × 4.*
3 and 4 are called a pair of factors of 12.

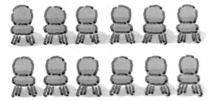

◄ *12 chairs can also be arranged in 2 rows of 6.*
12 = 2 × 6.
2 and 6 are another pair of factors of 12.

◄ *12 chairs can be arranged in 1 row of 12.*
12 = 1 × 12.
1 and 12 are a third pair of factors of 12.

12 has three pairs of factors: 1 × 12, 2 × 6, 3 × 4
and it has 6 factors: 1, 2, 3, 4, 6, 12.

Some pairs of factors can be seen on the **multiplication square**.

To find some pairs of factors of 20, for example, look for the position of 20 on the square.

This gives: 2 × 10, 4 × 5 and 5 × 4.

Notice that another pair, 1 × 20, does not appear on the square, unless you extend the square.

1	2	3	4	5	6	7	8	9	10
2	4	6	8	10	12	14	16	18	20
3	6	9	12	15	18	21	24	27	30
4	8	12	16	20	24	28	32	36	40
5	10	15	20	25	30	35	40	45	50
6	12	18	24	30	36	42	48	54	60
7	14	21	28	35	42	49	56	63	70
8	16	24	32	40	48	56	64	72	80
9	18	27	36	45	54	63	72	81	90
10	20	30	40	50	60	70	80	90	100

Use your head

Use the multiplication square to find some pairs of factors of: **24, 30, 25**

Prime numbers

You can list the **factors** of numbers in a table:

Number	Factor pairs	Factors
1	1×1	1
2	1×2	1, 2
3	1×3	1, 3
4	1×4, 2×2	1, 2, 4
5	1×5	1, 5
6	1×6, 2×3	1, 2, 3, 6
7	1×7	1, 7
8	1×8, 2×4	1, 2, 4, 8
9	1×9, 3×3	1, 3, 9
10	1×10, 2×5	1, 2, 5, 10
11	1×11	1, 11
12	1×12, 2×6, 3×4	1, 2, 3, 4, 6, 12
13	1×13	1, 13
14	1×14, 2×7	1, 2, 7, 14
15	1×15, 3×5	1, 3, 5, 15
16	1×16, 2×8, 4×4	1, 2, 4, 8, 16
17	1×17	1, 17
18	1×18, 2×9, 3×6	1, 2, 3, 6, 9, 18
19	1×19	1, 19
20	1×20, 2×10, 4×5	1, 2, 4, 5, 10, 20
..	....	....

◀ *Notice that some numbers have several factors, and some have not very many.*

What does it mean?

Numbers which have exactly 2 factors are called **prime numbers**.
Check that the prime numbers in the list are: 2, 3, 5, 7, 11, 13, 17, 19.

Notice that they are all odd numbers, except for one of them.
2 is the only even prime number.

24

You can find prime numbers by using an ancient method known as the Sieve of Eratosthenes. Eratosthenes was a Greek mathematician. His method sifts out all the numbers which are not prime, leaving all the prime numbers in the sieve.

▶ *To find the prime numbers up to 100, there are 5 stages:*

1. *Place a counter on 1.*
2. *Place counters on all the **multiples** of 2, except 2 itself.*
3. *Place counters on all the multiples of 3, except 3 itself.*
4. *Place counters on all the multiples of 5, except 5 itself.*
5. *Place counters on all the multiples of 7, except 7 itself.*

The numbers left over are the prime numbers.

1	2	3	4	5	6	7	8	9	10
11	12	13	14	15	16	17	18	19	20
21	22	23	24	25	26	27	28	29	30
31	32	33	34	35	36	37	38	39	40
41	42	43	44	45	46	47	48	49	50
51	52	53	54	55	56	57	58	59	60
61	62	63	64	65	66	67	68	69	70
71	72	73	74	75	76	77	78	79	80
81	82	83	84	85	86	87	88	89	90
91	92	93	94	95	96	97	98	99	100

These are the prime numbers up to 100:

2 3 5 7 11 13 17 19 23 29 31 37 41
43 47 53 59 61 67 71 73 79 83 89 97

Play the prime number game

This is a game for two players. Take turns to throw two dice to make a two-digit number. For example, if you throw a 2 and 3, you can make 23 or 32. You collect a counter for every prime number you can make. The winner is the first to collect 8 counters.

Square numbers

▲ *Each set of stamps is in a square arrangement.*
Count the number of stamps in each.
The smallest is 1, then 4, then 9, and so on...
The numbers are: 1, 4, 9, 16, 25, 36, 49, 64, 81, 100
*These numbers are called **square numbers**.*

What does it mean?

A square number is the result of multiplying a number by itself:

$1 \times 1 = 1$

$2 \times 2 = 4$

$3 \times 3 = 9$

$4 \times 4 = 16$

$5 \times 5 = 25$

$6 \times 6 = 36$

$7 \times 7 = 49$

$8 \times 8 = 64$

$9 \times 9 = 81$

$10 \times 10 = 100$

1	2	3	4	5	6	7	8	9	10
2	4	6	8	10	12	14	16	18	20
3	6	9	12	15	18	21	24	27	30
4	8	12	16	20	24	28	32	36	40
5	10	15	20	25	30	35	40	45	50
6	12	18	24	30	36	42	48	54	60
7	14	21	28	35	42	49	56	63	70
8	16	24	32	40	48	56	64	72	80
9	18	27	36	45	54	63	72	81	90
10	20	30	40	50	60	70	80	90	100

▲ *The square numbers all lie along the* **diagonal** *of a* **multiplication square**.

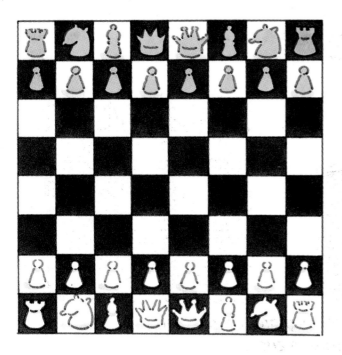

◀ A chessboard has 64 squares.
It is an 8 x 8 square.
Each player starts with
16 (= 4 × 4) pieces.

▶ The number of pins
on a square pinboard
is a square number.

Square number	Factors
1	1
4	1, 2, 4
9	1, 3, 9
16	1, 2, 4, 8, 16
25	1, 5, 25
36	1, 2, 3, 4, 6, 9, 12, 18, 36
49	1, 7, 49
64	1, 2, 4, 8, 16, 32, 64
81	1, 3, 9, 27, 81
100	1, 2, 4, 5, 10, 20, 25, 50, 100

◀ All square numbers
have an odd number
of factors.

Fun to do

Use a set of numbered cards 0 to
9. See how many different square
numbers you can lay out with the
ten cards. For example 4, 16, 25 are
three square numbers, and use
1, 2, 4, 5, 6.

Can you show more than three?

Special numbers

We find certain numbers everywhere in our lives. These can be called special numbers.

4 is a special number. Here are some of the reasons why it is special. It is special because it is:

- *the number of legs on an animal*
- *the number of seasons in a year*
- *the number of suits in a a pack of cards*
- *the number of wings on a bee*
- *the number of sides and **vertices** (corners) of a square*
- *the number of holes in many buttons.*

The word 'four' has 4 letters. It is the only one of our numbers which matches its number of letters.

There are lots of other properties of the number 4. It is:

- an even number
- a multiple of 2
- a factor of 20
- a **square number**.

5 is a special number, because it is:

- *the number of fingers on a hand*
- *the number of toes on a foot*
- *the number of sides and vertices of a **pentagon***
- *the number of vowels in the alphabet*
- *the number of petals on some flowers*
- *the number of players in a basketball team.*

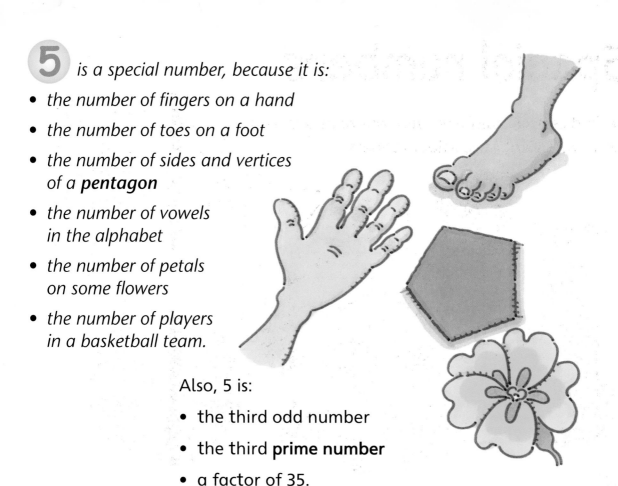

Also, 5 is:

- the third odd number
- the third **prime number**
- a factor of 35.

Here are some reasons why **6** is special:

- the number of sides and vertices of a **hexagon**
- the number of months in half a year
- the number of legs on an insect
- the number of faces on a cube or **cuboid**.

Use your head

Nearly all numbers are special in some way.

Can you think of two reasons why each of these numbers is special?

 7 **30** **12** **3**

Glossary

abacus	piece of apparatus to show numbers and to calculate with numbers
approximation	rough guess at the size of a number or calculation
centimetre	small unit for measuring length
common multiples	the common multiples of two numbers are multiples of both
cuboid	solid (3-D) shape; a box shape with rectangles as sides
decimal number	a number which has a whole number part and a fraction part. Each part is separated by a decimal point.
decimal point	a point used to separate the whole numbers from the fraction in a decimal number
denominator	bottom number in a fraction
diagonal	line drawn from one corner (vertex) of a shape to an opposite corner
digit	a symbol 0 to 9, used to write a number
equivalent	the same or equal amount
equivalent fractions	different fractions which have the same value even though they have different numerators and denominators
estimate	a good guess using what you know or understand
factors	factors of a number are numbers which will divide exactly into the number
fifth	when something is divided into five equal parts, each part is one fifth
fraction	part of a whole
fraction wall	chart to show equivalent fractions
half	when something is divided into two equal parts, each part is one half

hexagon	flat (2-D) shape with 6 straight sides
minus	subtraction sign '−' short for 'take away' or 'subtract'
multiples	the multiples of a number are the numbers in its multiplication table
multiplication square	a 10 by 10 square showing the results of all the multiplication facts up to 10×10
negative number	a number less than zero
number line	line with 'divisions' or markings which are numbered in order
numerator	the top number in a fraction
pentagon	flat (2-D) shape with 5 straight sides
per cent	out of a hundred. Also written as %.
percentage	a number of hundredths of a whole
plus	addition sign '+' short for 'add'
positive number	a number more than zero
prime number	a number with exactly two factors, itself and 1
quarter	when something is divided into four equal parts, each part is one quarter
rounding	you round a number when you say the rough size of a number
square numbers	when a number is multiplied by itself the result is a square number
temperature	a measure of how hot or cold something is
third	when something is divided into three equal parts, each part is one third
vertex	the corner of a 2-D or a 3-D shape; the plural is vertices

Answers

Page 4
Use your head 40; 600
Question two-digit; four-digit; three-digit; six-digit

Page 5
Use your head
125; 152; 127; 172; 157; 175; 215; 251; 217; 271; 257; 275; 512; 521; 517; 571; 527; 572; 712; 721; 715; 751; 725; 752

Page 7
Use your head
$72 \rightarrow 100; 70$
$323 \rightarrow 300; 320$
$178 \rightarrow 200; 180$

Page 8
Question halves; quarters; thirds; fifths; sixths; fifths
Question quarters; thirds; eigths; halves

Page 9
Use your head 6; 4; 3; 2; 1

Page 11
Use your head three quarters, $\frac{3}{4}$; two thirds $\frac{2}{3}$; five sixths $\frac{5}{6}$; two fifths $\frac{2}{5}$; four ninths $\frac{4}{9}$; three eighths $\frac{3}{8}$; nine tenths $\frac{9}{10}$; one twelfth $\frac{1}{12}$

Use your head happy: $\frac{5}{8}$; sad: $\frac{3}{8}$; wearing a hat: $\frac{5}{8}$
not wearing a hat: $\frac{3}{8}$
wearing a moustache: $\frac{4}{8} = \frac{1}{2}$;
not wearing a moustache: $\frac{4}{8} = \frac{1}{2}$;
wearing glasses: $\frac{1}{8}$;
not wearing glasses: $\frac{7}{8}$

Page 12
Use your head $\frac{2}{4} = \frac{1}{2}$; $\frac{4}{8} = \frac{1}{2}$; $\frac{2}{8} = \frac{1}{4}$; $\frac{6}{8} = \frac{3}{4}$;
$\frac{2}{2}$ = one whole;
$\frac{4}{4}$ = one whole;
$\frac{8}{8}$ = one whole

Page 13
Use your head For example:
$\frac{2}{3} = \frac{4}{6}$; $\frac{3}{5} = \frac{6}{10}$; $\frac{3}{4} = \frac{6}{8}$; $\frac{1}{6} = \frac{2}{12}$; $\frac{4}{5} = \frac{8}{10}$

Page 15
Use your head thirty four and six tenths, thirty four point six; three and seven tenths, three point seven; one and forty two hundredths, one and four tenths and two hundredths, one point four two; ten and thirty five hundredths, ten and three tenths and five hundredths, ten point three five

Page 16
Use your head 3 letters: 28%; 4 letters: 16%

Page 19
Use your head Vienna: −2°C; Paris: 9°C; Moscow: −8°C; Madrid: 6°C; Budapest: −5°C
Use your head Billie; My present; Crazy Baby

Page 21
Question 6; 12; 18

Page 23
Use your head
24: 1×24, 2×12, 3×8, 4×6;
30: 1×30, 2×15, 3×10, 5×6;
25: 1×25, 5×5

Page 29
Use your head Suggestions:
7: number of days in a week, prime number, odd number;
30: number of days in April, multiple of 5, half of 60;
12: dozen, number of months in a year, half of 24;
3: prime number, odd number, number of sides in a triangle

Index